SHARKS

Design
David West
Children's Book Design
Illustrations
Louise Nevett
Tessa Barwick
Picture Research
Cecilia Weston-Baker
Editor
Kate Petty

© Aladdin Books Ltd 1989
Designed and produced by
Aladdin Books Ltd
28 Percy Street
London W1P 9FF

*First Published in
Great Britain in 1988 by*
Franklin Watts
96 Leonard Street
London EC2A 4RH

First paperback edition published 1991

Hardback ISBN 0 86313 585 4
Paperback ISBN 0 07496 0673 8

Printed in Belgium

This book tells you about sharks — how they live, what they look like and how they survive in the ocean today. Find out some surprising facts in the boxes on each page. The Identification Chart at the back will help you when you see sharks in the zoo or aquaria.

 or

The little square shows you the size of the shark. Each side represents about three metres.

A red square means that a shark is being studied by scientists. Turn to the Survival File.

The picture opposite is a White-tip Shark photographed in the Red Sea

FIRST SIGHT
SHARKS

Alwyne Wheeler

GLOUCESTER PRESS
London · New York · Toronto · Sydney

Introduction

There were plenty of sharks in the sea 350 million years ago, long before mammals, birds or other fishes were common. So sharks are survivors of the prehistoric age, ideally suited to the world they live in. There are about 340 different kinds of shark known today. Many of them are magnificent creatures.

Like all other animals, sharks need to be protected – perhaps more so, because so few people like them. In fact, most sharks live far out to sea and are unlikely to attack a human.

Scientists are trying to find out more about sharks. Bathers might be able to avoid attack if they understand why sharks behave in a certain way.

Contents
Streamlined for speed **7**
Non-stop swimmers **8**
Extra senses **11**
Teeth for biting **12**
Unfussy diet **15**
Fellow travellers **17**
Gentle giants **19**
Unsafe waters **20**
Strange sharks **23**
Shark babies **24**
Sharks' enemies **27**
Survival file **28**
Identification chart **30**
Draw a life-size shark **30**
Index **32**

◁ **Close encounter with a Blue Shark**

Streamlined for speed

Sharks are perfectly built for life in the sea. Their streamlined shape and the way in which the high tail fin is balanced by the pectoral fins means that they can swim and dive effortlessly. Their long tails drive them along at a gentle cruising speed. When hunting they can travel at about 35 kph to catch fast-swimming animals such as squids, anchovies and flying fishes.

Many sharks, like the Blue Shark, are powerful long-distance swimmers too. Blue Sharks are found all round the world where the sea is warm. In summertime they follow the warmer water. Blue Sharks live near the surface. The clear blue of their backs and pure white colouring of the underside are typical of sharks which live near the surface of the sea.

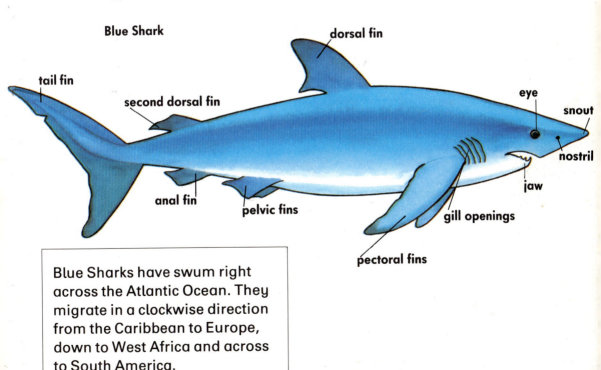

Blue Sharks have swum right across the Atlantic Ocean. They migrate in a clockwise direction from the Caribbean to Europe, down to West Africa and across to South America.

◁ A Blue Shark, perfect swimming machine

Non-stop swimmers

Active sharks which live near the surface of the sea, like the White-tip Shark, keep moving all their lives. They never stop swimming and go to sleep. Sharks that live on the seabed may lie still for hours on end. Some may find underwater caves in which they can snooze. Unlike most fishes, sharks do not have an air bladder to help them float. Instead they have a large oily liver which does the same job.

Sharks get a constant supply of oxygen when they swim continuously. A steady stream of water flows over their gills and out of the five gill slits on each side of the head. The gills extract oxygen from the water. If the shark stops swimming or is trapped, the water no longer flows over its gills. Then it cannot take in oxygen and it drowns.

White-tip Shark

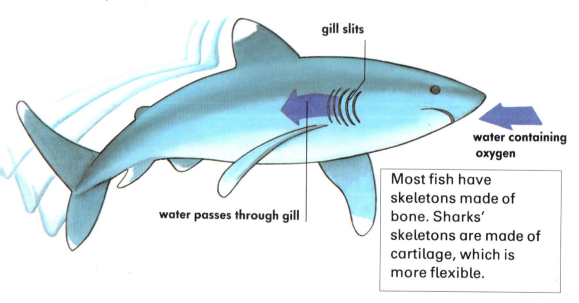

Most fish have skeletons made of bone. Sharks' skeletons are made of cartilage, which is more flexible.

The White-tip Shark is probably the most common of the big sharks in the open sea ▷

Extra senses

Sharks depend very heavily on smell to find their food. Their nostrils are quite large and far apart. When searching for food sharks swing their heads from side to side and turn to where they smell the strongest scent. Scientists think that sharks sometimes bump an object to "taste" it through taste cells in the skin. Incredibly sensitive cells on a shark's snout pick up the tiniest electrical discharges from a nearby animal. They can also feel vibrations along the sensitive "lateral line" when an animal is struggling in the water. On top of all this, they can smell blood in the water even when it is diluted ten million times. So they do not depend on their eyesight to hunt their prey.

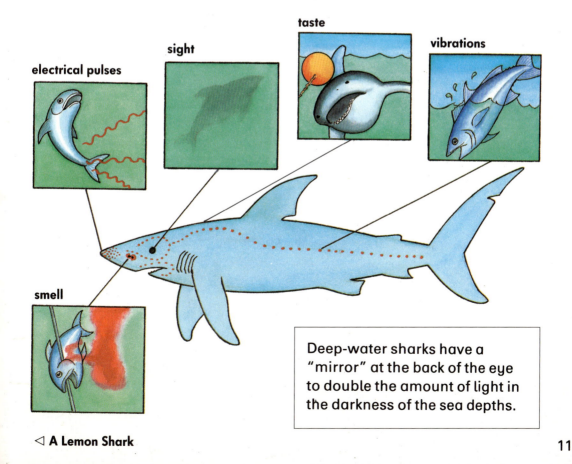

Deep-water sharks have a "mirror" at the back of the eye to double the amount of light in the darkness of the sea depths.

◁ **A Lemon Shark**

Teeth for biting

Sharks never stop growing new teeth. All of them have many rows of teeth in both jaws. As the front ones wear down and fall out they are replaced by new teeth from inside the jaw. The Lemon Shark replaces about 30 teeth each week.

The shape of a shark's teeth depends on the food it eats. The Tiger Shark often eats turtles. It has saw-edged teeth in both jaws. It bites the turtle and then shakes its head slowly from side to side so that the teeth saw through the shell and bones. The Port Jackson Shark has large, flat teeth for crushing sea-urchins, prawns and crabs. The Nurse Shark uses its heavy jaws for crushing shellfish while its hundreds of small, pointed teeth hold the food still.

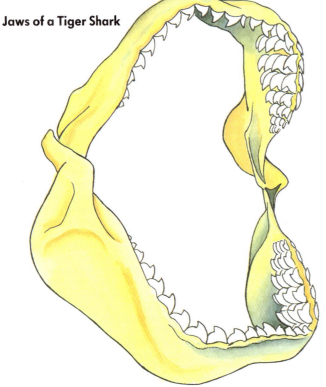

Jaws of a Tiger Shark

The power of a shark's bite is immense – a pressure of 3,000 kg per square centimetre compared with a human bite of 10 kg per square centimetre.

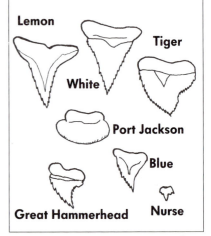

Lemon

Tiger

White

Port Jackson

Blue

Great Hammerhead

Nurse

A Sand Tiger Shark showing its teeth ▷

Unfussy diet

Most active sharks have sharp-edged or spiky teeth. They feed on many different kinds of prey. Some, like the Blue Shark, eat fast-swimming squids and all kinds of fishes which live in the surface waters. Other sharks, like the Tiger Shark, seem to eat almost anything they come across – dolphins, sea mammals, seabirds and turtles. Fishermen have found old boots, tin cans, beef bones, floats from fishing nets, the head of a sheep and even a dead dog inside Tiger Sharks. Much of this was rubbish dumped in the sea. It is easy to see why the Tiger Shark has been called the dustbin of the sea!

When several sharks pick up the scent of blood they rush in to bite at the prey in a "feeding frenzy".

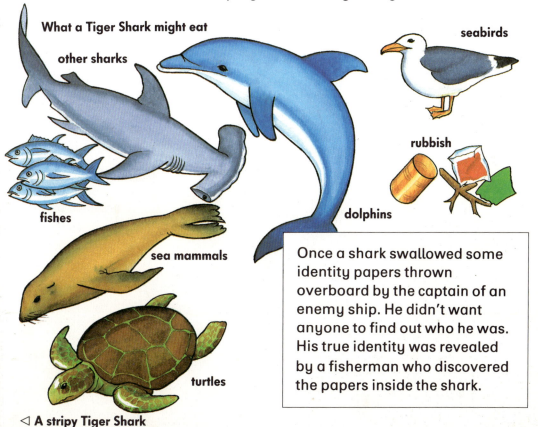

What a Tiger Shark might eat — other sharks, fishes, sea mammals, turtles, dolphins, seabirds, rubbish

Once a shark swallowed some identity papers thrown overboard by the captain of an enemy ship. He didn't want anyone to find out who he was. His true identity was revealed by a fisherman who discovered the papers inside the shark.

◁ A stripy Tiger Shark

Fellow travellers

Sometimes sharks travel in groups but often they hunt alone. Even those lone hunters are usually accompanied by smaller fishes which swim close by. Pilot fishes have dark stripes across their bodies. They hide in the shadow of the shark, protected from their enemies but able to dart out and snap up any suitable food.

Shark suckers and remoras are sucker fish which actually hitch a ride on the shark. They cling to its rough skin by a sucker on top of the head and back. They usually stay close to the shark, feeding on any parasites that attach themselves to it. They also feed on small creatures passing by.

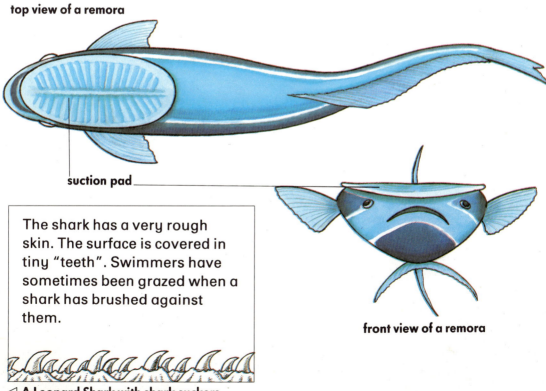

top view of a remora

suction pad

The shark has a very rough skin. The surface is covered in tiny "teeth". Swimmers have sometimes been grazed when a shark has brushed against them.

front view of a remora

◁ **A Leopard Shark with shark suckers**

Gentle giants

Three kinds of very large shark are harmless, slow-moving giants. The Whale Shark, the biggest known shark at 13.7 metres long, lives in tropical seas. It swims along sucking in minute animal plankton. Sometimes it feeds on anchovies, sardines and other small fishes.

Basking Sharks live in cooler, temperate seas and grow up to about 10 metres. They feed on animal plankton by swimming along with their mouths open.

Megamouth has only been found twice. It grows to 4.5 metres. It lives in deep water and feeds only on deep-sea shrimps. They are attracted by light organs that glow inside its huge mouth.

▽ **A Basking Shark with its mouth open**

◁ **A Whale Shark**

A Great White Shark ▷

Unsafe waters

Sometimes swimmers are killed by sharks. Altogether there are around 100 shark attacks on people each year, but only about 25 to 30 of the victims actually die. Almost all attacks take place in the warm waters around the coasts of Australia, South Africa and the warmer coasts of North America. This is partly because the heat seems to make the sharks more aggressive.

Only about 20 kinds of sharks are dangerous. The most dangerous of all is probably the Great White Shark. It grows to at least 6.4 metres, large enough to eat seals, sealions, porpoises and big fishes as well as occasional swimmers. Most sharks attack when they are frightened or threatened by a swimmer's approach rather than because they are hungry.

Sharks are attracted by splashing and struggling. If a shark is near by, a swimmer should swim away strongly and steadily and try not to panic.

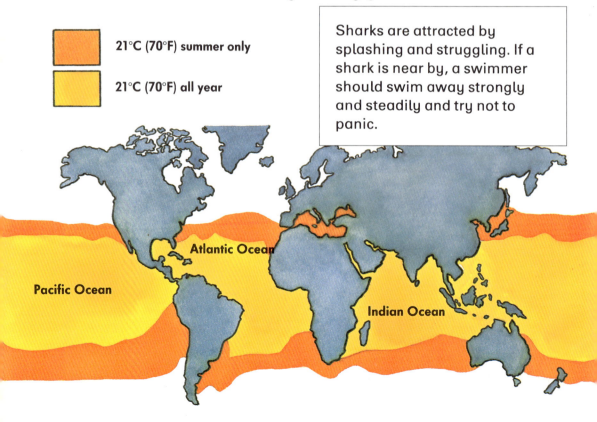

21°C (70°F) summer only

21°C (70°F) all year

Pacific Ocean

Atlantic Ocean

Indian Ocean

Strange sharks

Hammerhead Sharks have their heads flattened and sideways to form a hammer shape. They have an enormous advantage over other sharks. The eyes at the extreme ends of the hammer are able to see all round the shark and their widely-spaced nostrils help them smell food at a great distance. Hammerheads are usually the first sharks to arrive at a bait.

The Wobbegong lives on the coasts of northern Australia and Papua New Guinea, usually close to coral reefs. Its mottled colouring and long fringed beard around its head help it to hide amongst seaweeds and coral. It lies in wait for fishes, crabs, lobsters or octopuses to come close enough to catch.

▽ **A Wobbegong Shark lying near the seabed**

◁ **The strange Hammerhead Shark**

Shark babies

Most fishes lay their eggs in the water, but sharks do not just abandon their eggs. Many shark babies are kept inside the mother's body until they are big enough to swim and feed on their own. The Blue Shark sometimes has as many as 50 babies at a time, but others, like the Porbeagle, have only one or two. A spurdog carries her 20 babies inside her for nearly two years before they are born.

The Dogfish – a small shark – lays its eggs in small leathery cases. They have long threads at the corners to tangle in seaweed and stop them being washed away. The baby Dogfish hatches out after 5-11 months when it is about 10 centimetres in length.

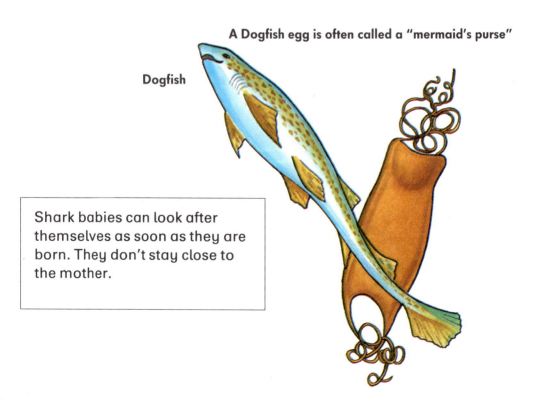

A Dogfish egg is often called a "mermaid's purse"

Dogfish

Shark babies can look after themselves as soon as they are born. They don't stay close to the mother.

A young Port Jackson Shark ▷

◁ **This Blue Shark has been caught by fishermen for sport**

Sharks' enemies

Because many sharks are large and can swim quickly there are very few animals which attack them. Some small or newborn sharks are eaten by bigger sharks, and some are attacked by Orca Whales, Sperm Whales and large fishes. A number of dolphins will attack a shark together to protect their own young. Swordfish have also been known to stab at sharks.

The biggest enemy of sharks is man. About 30 people a year are killed by sharks, but about 4.5 million sharks are killed by people. In some countries sharks like the Dogfish and the Spurdog are used for food.

Dolphins sometimes attack sharks

Several kinds of small shark are sold in English fish shops. They are usually called flake or rock-eel.

Survival file

Sharks have survived for millions of years. But even though their ocean habitat is not in any particular danger, they are at risk from the activities of humans who see them as an evil menace. Luckily, there are scientists who want to study sharks and find out more about them. The best place to watch sharks is in their natural surroundings. Divers sometimes stay inside a cage so they cannot be attacked. Then they can film the sharks at close quarters in safety. They attract the sharks with a bait of fresh fish.

Filming a Great White Shark from a cage

Experienced divers sometimes swim freely among the sharks. They carry a stick with an explosive head on it to stave off the dangerous sharks. They try to understand the sharks' "body language". The way a shark moves when it is swimming towards a diver may tell us whether it is aggressive, frightened, curious, hungry or even playful. Divers "tag" sharks by fastening a number on to a fin. If one is recaptured they can see how it has grown and how far it has travelled.

Diver alongside a Whale Shark

Valerie Taylor testing her shark-suit

Scientists can also learn from sharks kept in captivity. They are studying how they hear, how well they can see, and how much they depend on their sense of smell. They want to find out how the organs that detect faint electric discharges from other animals work. It is important to learn about their sense of taste. If scientists can find a substance that sharks do not like, then swimmers and divers will be able to carry it with them in case of attack.

Some naturalists, like the Taylors, find sharks so fascinating that they have made them a lifetime's study.

Identification chart

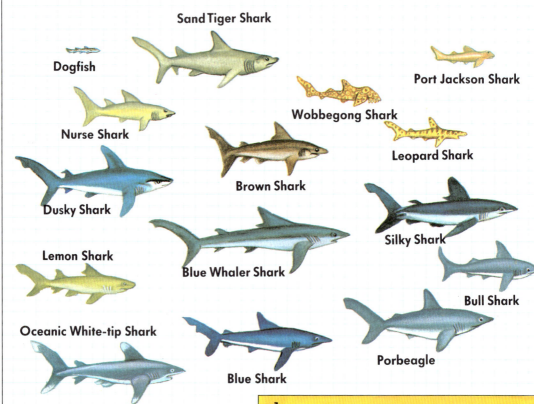

This chart shows you some of the more common sharks. You can see some of them in the zoo. The sharks are drawn to scale to show their comparative sizes.

Sand Tiger Shark
Dogfish
Port Jackson Shark
Wobbegong Shark
Nurse Shark
Leopard Shark
Brown Shark
Dusky Shark
Silky Shark
Lemon Shark
Blue Whaler Shark
Bull Shark
Oceanic White-tip Shark
Porbeagle
Blue Shark

Draw a life-size shark
1 Make yourself a huge sheet of paper.
2 Divide it into (roughly) 30-centimetre squares.
3 Copy your shark from these pages, using the squares here to help you.
4 Colour in your shark.
5 Cut it out carefully.
6 You can mount it on stiff card.

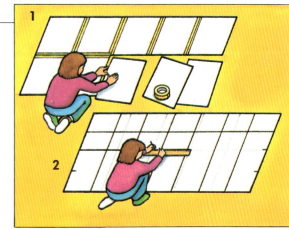

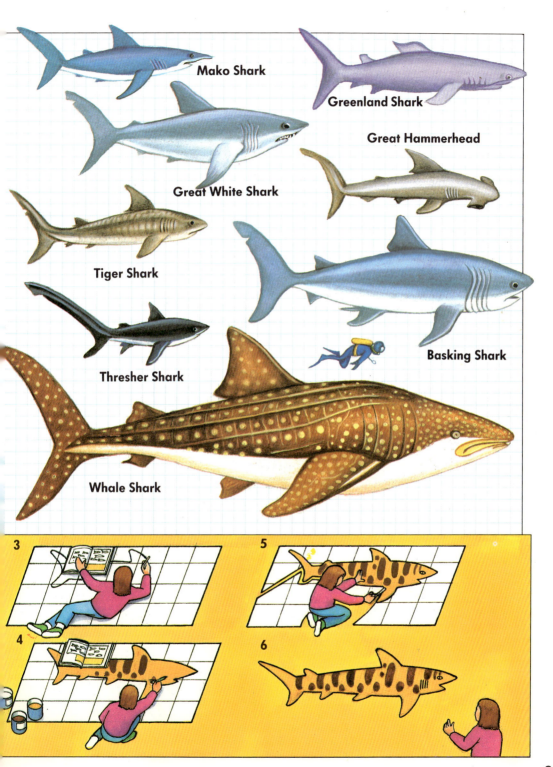

Index

A attacks 20

B babies 24
Basking Shark 19, 31
Blue Shark 7, 12, 15, 24, 29, 30

D Dogfish 24, 27, 30

F feeding frenzy 15

G gills 8
Great White Shark 20, 21, 31

H Hammerhead 12, 22, 31

L lateral line 11
Lemon Shark 12, 30
Leopard Shark 16, 30

M Mako Shark 12, 31
Megamouth 19

N Nurse Shark 12, 30

P pilot fish 17
Porbeagle 24, 30
Port Jackson Shark 12, 25, 30

R remora 17

S Sand Tiger Shark 30
Spurdog 24, 27, 30

T tagging 29
teeth 12
Tiger Shark 12, 15, 31

W Whale Shark 18, 19, 31
White-tip Shark 8, 30
Wobbegong Shark 23, 30

The picture on the cover shows a Great White Shark

Photographic credits: Cover, title page, contents page and pages 9, 16, 18, 19, 25, 30 and 31 (top): Planet Earth; pages 6, 14, 21, 22 and 31 (bottom): Ardea; pages 10 and 26: Zefa; page 13: Frank Lane Agency; page 23: Bruce Coleman.